My Guide Inside®

Knowing Myself and Understanding My World
(Book III)
Teacher's Manual
for Advanced, Secondary MGI Learner Book

Christa Campsall
with
Kathy Marshall Emerson

3 Principles Ed Talks
ed-talks.com

First Printing, 2017
Printed in the United States of America
Authored With: Kathy Marshall Emerson
Conceptual Development: Barbara Aust, Kathy Marshall Emerson
Production: Tom Tucker
Graphic Design: Josephine Aucoin
Webmaster: Michael Campsall

Contents

Promise of Change

Outcomes: What Teens Report..iv

Foreword..v

Objectives of *My Guide Inside*..vi

Encouragement to Teachers..1

Overview for Teaching *My Guide Inside*

Curriculum Foundations in Research 2

Suggestions for Using *My Guide Inside*...3

Digital Media Options and Video Clips 5

Introduction to Lesson Plans 5

Learner Pre- and Post-Assessments...6

Teacher "Snapshot" Learner Observations 7

Evaluation Rating Scales for Lesson Activities 9

Lesson Plans

Learning the Foundation

Chapter 1 - Discovering *My Guide Inside*..12

Chapter 2 - The Lure of Being Secure 15

Learning From Life

Chapter 3 - Flawsome and Fun: Our True Identity 18

Chapter 4 - Living in the Present: Leaving the Past in the Dust 21

Chapter 5 - Understanding the Lost Thinker 24

Chapter 6 - Making Room for Happiness 27

Chapter 7 - Facing the Future in a State of Well-being 30

Moving Forward

Chapter 8 - Defining Your Individual Path 33

Integrating *MGI* in Education

My Guide Inside Meets Educational Learning Objectives, Competencies 36

Current Education Policy Context...36

Objectives of *My Guide Inside*...37

Educational Learning Objectives and Competencies

- English Language Arts Competencies 37

- Communication Competency...38

- Health, Career, and Personal, Social, Health & Economic Education 38

- Personal Well-being & Social Competencies 38

- Thinking Competency..39

Understanding Teens Today 39

MGI Learning Opportunities Designed for Teens..41

References Cited...42

Supplemental Resources

Sharing the Principles of Mind, Consciousness, and Thought..43

Recommended Three Principles Resources...45

Continued Learning for Educators 45

MGI in Context of Education Theory and Related Research 47

Acknowledgments...52

About the Author...53

About *MGI*

Overview of *My Guide Inside* Comprehensive Curriculum..53

What Professionals Say About *My Guide Inside* 54

Outcomes: What Teens Report

Real teens, aged 13-19, whom we have been privileged to work with,
describe their experiences learning the principles MGI explores:

❖ "I was surprised that the solutions to the situations we talked about actually worked!"

❖ "I got suspended before I found out some of this … I actually punched a kid … But then I found out it was a separate reality thing and it could've been stopped."

❖ "This class has helped me a lot. I have enjoyed it. I hope we can do it next year. This class will help me all the way through my life. Thank you."

❖ "This school course has helped me a lot with dealing with my family. We didn't get along very well and now I have more patience and my temper doesn't flare up as much as it used to. We still disagree a lot but we actually talk now and don't fight at all. We never used to talk, unless we were fighting, but now we sit in the same room and actually talk about how our day was and our plans for the rest of the day or the week."

❖ "Many people run all their lives looking for happiness. During this course, I found that having a main objective of inner peace helped me to see my way clear. When I'm thinking negatively and being bummed out, I take time to think about inner peace and I use it as a centering point. Having this way of centering myself has shown to be helpful. It was always hard for me to relax and be peaceful inside. By recognizing inner peace, it's easier for me to relax."

❖ "I used quiet mind because I didn't do any of my homework and I had a ton to do the next day. So I did it all in school. Just kind of calmed myself down at the end of the day and did a bunch. Got it all done. I was proud of myself."

❖ "The most valuable aspect of the course would have to be learning about Thought and state of mind because I now know that thoughts are what you make them. It also has helped me to stop analyzing negative thoughts and [to learn] how to prevent them by being positive. It works. Thanks!"

❖ "I learned about Three Principles in school about 15 years ago and this knowledge is still the foundation of my life today!" (From a former teen, now an adult)

Foreword

If you are reading this book, you and your students are beginning an extraordinary life-changing process. I am a psychiatrist old enough to be the grandfather of your students. I would like to share a very personal message with you.

I had to stumble and bumble through my teenage years doing the best I could with limited understanding of my true nature. I did not know how my moment-to-moment experience was created. I had no clue wisdom was available to guide me through all the challenges in my life.

I spent 26 years in school to become a psychiatrist, but I did not learn about true mental health. For many years while I was treating patients I was personally depressed.

But just like you, I got lucky! I had the opportunity to learn the Three Principles and my life and clinical practice changed forever. Trust me, having the three universal principles of Mind, Thought and Consciousness shared with your students, which is the purpose of *My Guide Inside*, is the most precious and life changing gift possible!

These universal principles will introduce your students to their true nature and the inside-out nature of experience. *My Guide Inside* points students to the ever-present internal guidance of wisdom. For the rest of their lives whenever they are faced with challenges and uncertainties these lessons will be PRICELESS!

When I was six and my brother was three, he took his hands off the glass Coca Cola bottle and grabbed the straw in the bottle. He watched with surprise, dismay and confusion as the bottle and its contents went crashing and splashing to the floor. I have never forgotten the principle of gravity.

I share this, as a man, who traversed the teenage years himself; as a father, who helped raise four children; and as a psychiatrist with more than 40 years of experience and Board Certification in Adolescent Psychiatry, who assisted a multitude of adolescent clients in their journey to adulthood. For that reason, I have written the personal message to your students located in the Learner Book. Understanding principles of mental health makes a difference, too!!! Thank you for guiding your students on the journey to happiness!

Dr. William (Bill) Pettit, MD
Psychiatrist

Objectives of My Guide Inside

The principles Dr. Pettit refers to operate in all people, including every teen. This *MGI* curriculum points the way to wholeness, happiness, creativity and well-being in all parts of every student's life.

Therefore, *MGI* has these two academic goals for students: (1) to enhance Personal Well-being with an understanding of these principles, and (2) to develop competencies in Communication, Thinking, and Personal and Social Responsibility. *MGI* accomplishes both goals by using stories, discussion and various written and creative activities, as the learning increases your students' competency in English Language Arts, including Digital Media.

Discovering the personal *Guide Inside*, key to learning, enhances student ability to make decisions, navigate life and build healthy relationships. Accessing natural wisdom will affect their well-being, spiritual wellness, personal and social responsibility, and positive personal and cultural identity. Social and emotional learning, including self-determination, self-regulation and self-efficacy, are also natural outcomes of greater awareness.

Encouragement to Teachers

Welcome to a wonderful new experience sharing the principles Dr. Pettit talks about, commonly called Three Principles, with your students. I have spent my entire teaching career introducing students and educators to these principles. The comments at the beginning and end of *MGI III* are from some of my students and professional colleagues. You can have the same kind of impact! Make the words in *My Guide Inside* come alive and use the teacher notes and lesson plans freely.

As a fellow teacher, I invite you, and indeed strongly encourage you to uncover your own *Guide Inside*. The words written here, as thoughtfully as they have been prepared for you and your learners, are only an "echo of truth."

Like everyone else in education I also had to find my way. I was a pre-service teacher in 1975 with an up-to-date skill set and a strong desire to help learners who were struggling. Still, I was reconsidering my career choice, because in spite of my desire, I could not reach learners with serious challenges. Try as I might, I could not reach kids.

What did make the difference? Hearing the truth of these principles. I came to understand the source of natural inner wisdom and well-being; my success rate reaching these learners soared. I had to find "the missing link" for myself, and thus began my lifelong learning journey focused on invigorating the intuitive mind – wisdom – my *Guide Inside*.

Knowing about this *Guide Inside* is valuable for all learners; however, it is particularly vital for struggling learners. They need knowledge and understanding to experience a healthy life. *My Guide Inside* for teens has amazing free digital media tools for every activity, as well as video clips to support the learning process for all teens. The curriculum is designed for your students with activities that can be graded to report on progress, however it is also designed for youth who are curious and whose investigation is not based on a need for grades.

As we learn these principles, we find there is no end to the inner wisdom that brings joy and compassion to life. As author Sydney Banks emphasizes, "Those who have found a balance between their intelligence and their innate wisdom are the lucky ones." (1998, p. 133) Let's be included with the lucky ones!

Make the words in *My Guide Inside* come alive; your success rate and satisfaction will increase profoundly. Ultimately, you will feel better as you experience a new world. As a colleague who wants to share what works without fail, I urge you to please access the included *Recommended Resources and Continued Learning for Educators* pages. Please, investigate. These resources are the foundation of *My Guide Inside*. Happy Teaching!

Warmest Regards,

Christa Campsall

Overview for Teaching My Guide Inside

As you prepare to share this curriculum with your students, there are some key considerations that can greatly enhance the support you receive from colleagues and administrators in your school system, and the impact you will have on your students. We have learned over the years the following information can be very beneficial.

❖ Curriculum Foundations in Research

Any responsible school curriculum must be built on a solid understanding of current educational research. There are many studies to be considered. For simplicity we have chosen to highlight one sample body of current significant research. (See "*MGI* in Context of Education Theory and Related Research" in this manual for a discussion and detailed listing of related scholarly publications.)

John Hattie holds a PhD from the University of Toronto and is Professor of Education and Director of the Education Research Institute at the University of Melbourne, Australia. He has also served as education professor, administrator, and research director in various universities in Canada, New Zealand, and the United States. He consults globally with key institutions and organizations. Dr. Hattie undertook the largest ever synthesis of meta-analyses of quantitative measures of the effect of different factors on educational outcomes. Hattie is widely published and most known for his Visible Learning books. His quantitative research methodologies document the influences on student achievement described below.

John Hattie and his team by 2015 studied over 1200 meta analyses related to influences on student achievement. These meta analyses examined more than 65,000 studies, 195,000 effect sizes and about ¼ billion students worldwide. Hattie aims to discover "what truly makes a difference in student learning." To answer this question Hattie identifies the greatest to the least "effect size" resulting from educational program, policy and innovation interventions.

In general, the Visible Learning massive global research story uncovered by John Hattie "argues that when teachers see teaching and learning through the eyes of their students, and when students become their own teachers the outcomes and engagement are maximized." (Hattie, 2015, pp. 70, 80.)

A recent report* with rankings, 1.62 to -.42, indicates these are the top three "effects sizes" impacting student achievement:

#1—Teacher estimates of student achievement 1.62
#2—Collective teacher efficacy 1.57
#3—Self-reported grades 1.33
When seen through a Three Principles lens, educators understand these effects this way:

#1— "Teacher estimates of student achievement" means an individual teacher's view that each student can achieve/learn; with the educator accurately seeing where a student is at present and then having insights revealing how to move the student forward. As Barb Aust writes, "There are no throw away" students and we reach them by "teaching in the moment." (Aust, 2013, 2016.)

#2— "Collective teacher efficacy" refers to educators in a school or team thinking—being confident—they can in fact be successful in teaching and reaching each and every student. They trust each other to add to the development of a solution.

#3— "Self-reported grades" indicates the degree to which a student knows that he or she is capable of successful learning which becomes self-fulfilling. When a student learns to drop, "I can't learn" thinking, intrinsic motivation propels the student. It is not surprising this effect ranks so highly.

Additionally, the most negative influence on student achievement is **Student Depression with -.42 effect size**. The impact of student well-being on academic achievement could not be clearer!

What makes a difference? Student's and teacher's thinking plays a critical role. For example, Hattie writes:

"It is less what teachers do in their teaching, but more how they think about their role. It is their mind frames or ways of thinking about teaching and learning that are most critical."

(Hattie, 2015, p. 81.)

The *My Guide Inside* curriculum, based on these principles, directs teachers and learners beyond believing into knowing this is true—that every student can learn and every teacher can discover insights and wisdom to guide effective teaching. Self-efficacy of both student and teacher come naturally when the inside-out nature of life is discovered.

---

* These rankings are visually available at www.visiblelearning.org/nvd3/visualize/hattie-ranking-interactive-2009-2011-2015.html. It is also important to realize as John Hattie's research continues indefinitely, the precise effect rankings and even definitions of effects will vary slightly. For example, in 2016 Jenni Donohoo describes collective teacher efficacy at 1.57 as the most influential effect (Donohoo, p. 6). Despite various interpretations, we feel key identified factors align well with our Three Principles understanding.

❖ **Suggestions for Using** *My Guide Inside*

This curriculum is designed for use in a school or home or wherever it is important to bring hope to learners. Book III offers stories and activities designed for student success in this context:

Reading Level: "Advanced Fluent" (age 13-19) usually high school
Flexibility: regular course or adapt or modify to suit individual learners
Settings: classroom, small group or individual
Design: inclusive of self-directed learners working independently
Digital Media: free digital media options and video clips are provided at
myguideinside.com

In general, the following points may be important to consider:

Lesson Time Frame

Most chapters are estimated to need two 40 minute sessions. There are two exceptions best covered in three sessions: Chapter 4 has a long story and Chapter 6 has a two-part story. These estimates accommodate reading and discussion, vocabulary building, reflection and journal writing. Any additional activities will need more time. A wide variety of engaging activities with free Digital Media options and video clips are offered at myguideinside.com.

Clearly each teacher needs to adapt this curriculum framework to fit time available in already packed school schedules. Our dream is for a stand-alone course for academic credit.

Flexibility

The biggest challenge all educators will face everywhere is time. Use *My Guide Inside* (*MGI*) curriculum as a unit within a course or as a full credit course, if time permits. It is important to know you can adapt this curriculum and use it as a resource in your real situation. The chapters can be used in any order that works for you. Understanding time restrictions, this resource is also designed for you to use any of chapters one through seven as a stand-alone lesson. The last chapter, however, is designed for review.

MGI's main objectives are to increase student personal well-being awareness and responsibility. Therefore class discussions foster learner discovery of their own innate inner wisdom--called my *Guide Inside* in this material. We can experience inner wisdom by sharing "Big Picture" ideas. This curriculum is meant as a springboard to discovery.

Notice your own reflections which may be particularly insightful and guiding as you head toward preparing the next lesson. As mentioned before, your own insights will lead to a deeper understanding of your *Guide Inside*. Remember it's the feeling … listen for that good feeling and follow it with your students.

Learning, Living, Sharing

This means bringing the feeling, the "essential curriculum," with you every day. In other words, "live the principles" by being in a natural state of service; sharing compassion, understanding and joy in your classroom. Once you are being that informally and naturally, you will be sharing the principles, via a positive feeling. This will enhance and make more powerful any formal sharing you are able to do using lessons with students.

I am grateful to my colleague Kathy Marshall Emerson, who has introduced Three Principles to literally hundreds of teachers, for clarifying the simplicity of this process. (See reference: *Educators Living in the Joy of Gratitude*; particularly Webinar 12) Also see the very helpful book by Barb Aust, *The Essential Curriculum*, in which she beautifully describes what the school and classroom climate is like when the principles are integrated into educational settings. Barb has experience learning, living, and sharing Three Principles during her entire career; she has always shared such wisdom in her roles as teacher, principal and pre-service teacher supervisor.

❖ Digital Media Options and Video Clips

Digital Media Options for the learning activities are accessible and easy for teens to use. Links to these are located in a special *MGI* website created just for you and your students at myguideinside.com. No access code is needed. Chapter and lesson-specific activities use free online resources that will intrigue your students, and support you as a busy educator. Video clips can be projected for the class, as well as enjoyed outside of class.

The *MGI* website includes appropriate word processing, cloud storage, audio feedback, note taking capacity; and tools for image and banner making, blogging, publishing, video and file sharing, podcasting, mind mapping, video production, and writing support. Each of these was carefully studied and tested.

 If it's acceptable in your jurisdiction you may want to have BYOD (Bring Your Own Device) days for the Digital Media activities, which are easily created with these amazing, free tech tools. You may appreciate this resource: "The Teacher's Guide to Tech." (2016). www.teachers-guidetotech.com.

❖ Introduction to Lesson Plans

The preceding pages of this Teacher Manual have described the "Big Picture" of effectively preparing for and teaching the principles to your students. The following lesson plans begin with an abstract of the main lesson topics. The *MGI Learner Book* itself provides stories, activities and resources specific to each lesson. Please direct students to the *MGI Chapter Resource Center* for the activity success criteria, digital media options and vocabulary to expand thinking and communication. No planning is needed, simply read through the logically organized chapter and proceed. Lessons are easy to use.

The plans provide details about how each specific chapter lesson can be aligned with student academic progress. The lesson plans do not spell out what to include in a lesson; that is fully provided in the *MGI Learner Book*. Lesson plans suggest how student academic progress will be accomplished and observed as you carry out the actual lessons. This design achieves an opportunity for teachers to be their own evaluators. As John Hattie so strongly encourages us, "Know thy impact!"

The Lesson Plans and the *MGI Learner Book* together offer a way of sharing the principles so that student learning in broad important areas—*MGI* objectives for Personal Well-being Awareness and Responsibility in several areas—will be achieved. Class sets of *MGI Learner Books* can be used year after year. Alternatively, whenever possible, it is optimal to provide an *MGI Learner Book* (print or eBook) for each student to keep and access for further exploration of the key elements.

❖ **Start and End with Evaluation**

Learner Pre- and Post-Assessments

Before beginning Chapter 1, students complete the Learner *MGI III* Pre-Assessment found in Appendix A of the *MGI* Learner Book. Students can discover how they see their own well-being and responsibility before beginning the lessons and document their own progress with the *MGI III* Post-Assessment at the end of the course. This self-evaluation captures student progress in the two broad *MGI* objectives:

<u>PERSONAL WELL-BEING AWARENESS</u>

I am happy with my life.
I am hopeful about my future.
I use common sense, inner wisdom, to guide me.
I remain peaceful and calm in challenging situations.
I recognize how my own decisions and actions affect me.
I am aware of and responsible for my own well-being.
I manage my stress.

<u>COMMUNICATION, THINKING, PERSONAL AND SOCIAL RESPONSIBILITY</u>

I communicate effectively in classroom group discussions with other students.
I clearly express myself in written class assignments.
I use digital media communication effectively.
I use social media to support and help others.
I am a capable learner.
I am able to get the "big picture" as I learn new things.
I have determination and motivation to explore new topics.
I see the logical results of my own thinking and actions.
I catch myself "going off" emotionally, am able to calm down, and return to good behavior.
I make responsible decisions with consideration for others and also myself.

I am friendly, kind and likable.
I listen to others with clarity, curiosity or compassion.
I am good at solving "people problems" between my friends. These relevant outcome measures are reviewed briefly at the end of lesson plans for each chapter. Student self-observation can invigorate such outcomes to become "usually" apparent in daily life.

By keeping a copy of each student's Pre- and Post-Assessments, development can be monitored and discussed individually with each learner. When possible, a school district research office staffer may develop an efficient computerized system for data collection, analysis and reporting to the classroom teacher. Both individual student and full class reports may be developed.

Teacher "Snapshot" Learner Observations

The following form allows you to quickly document individual student progress. First compare Pre- and Post- Assessments for each student, reflect and then record your main observations on this quick "Snapshot".

This "Snapshot" has four questions. Ideally you will have time with each student to learn his or her sense of personal progress and share your observations. The final class comparisons of this "Snapshot" are important to share with your school administrators and policy makers.

Teacher "Snapshot" Learner Observations

Prior to completing this form, review each student's progress based on a comparison of their Pre-to Post- Assessments. Reflect and then complete this "Snapshot" to record your main observations. Take time with each student to hear his or her sense of personal progress. Then share your observations. Learn from and encourage each other.

Name: _____   Date: _____

PERSONAL WELL-BEING AWARENESS

Rarely   1   2   3   4   5   Usually

Observations:

COMMUNICATION, THINKING, PERSONAL AND SOCIAL RESPONSIBILITY

Rarely   1   2   3   4   5   Usually

Observations:

RELEVANT STUDENT INFORMATION

School Attendance

Not Yet Within Expectations   1   2   3   4   5   Fully Meets Expectations

Classroom academic performance

Not Yet Within Expectations   1   2   3   4   5   Fully Meets Expectations

Social behavior in and out of classroom

Not Yet Within Expectations   1   2   3   4   5   Fully Meets Expectations

Participation in class

Not Yet Within Expectations   1   2   3   4   5   Fully Meets Expectations

Observations:

Evaluation Rating Scales for Lesson Activities

Evaluation criteria for specific MGI Book III Activities are designed to monitor student progress and are found at the end of each chapter in the "MGI Chapter Resource Center" of the Learner Book. These may be used independently by the student for self-evaluation, in consultation with the teacher, or only by the teacher.

Evaluation Scale:

5	Exceptionally good; clearly meets or exceeds all criteria
4	Very Good; meets all criteria and exceeds some criteria
3	Good; meets all criteria
2	Less than Acceptable; meets some criteria; provide support
1	Limited; meets few criteria, in progress; provide adaptations/modifications

Add to the Story and Think of a Time Criteria	5	4	3	2	1

- focused central idea
- meaningful text shows depth of thought
- logical sequence
- clear language and correct conventions
- engaging voice is evident

Art Criteria	5	4	3	2	1

- original and creative
- skillful use of materials
- expressive and detailed
- effective use of space

Banner Criteria	5	4	3	2	1

- clear and expressive
- accurate and neat
- effective use of space
- colorful

Belonging Map Criteria	5	4	3	2	1

- thoughtful
- shows links
- accurate
- relevant

Blog Criteria	5	4	3	2	1

- original ideas
- clearly expressed
- shows understanding
- enhancements with accurate citation

Fast Forward Profiling Criteria	5	4	3	2	1

- engaging headline
- concise summary and interests reveal personality
- experience (paid and unpaid)
- thoughtful goals

Interview Report Criteria	5	4	3	2	1

- interview engages viewer with relevant information
- write-up has clear central idea
- engaging and fluent
- clear and correct conventions

Journal Entry or Dream Theme Criteria	5	4	3	2	1

- use "I"
- shares thoughts and feelings
- shows insight
- shows connections

Listicle Criteria	5	4	3	2	1

- original
- clearly express ideas; images reinforce text
- correct conventions
- strong last line

Personal Metaphor Criteria	5	4	3	2	1

- strong images
- true qualities
- effective use of space
- precision

Persuasive Writing Criteria	5	4	3	2	1

- point of view stated boldly with convincing reasons
- organized logically
- correct conventions
- call for "action"

Poem Writing Criteria	5	4	3	2	1

- depth of thought
- organized
- vivid language
- creates a mood

Poster Criteria	5	4	3	2	1

- informative, neat
- effective use of space
- colorful; accurate

Public Service Announcement (PSA) Criteria	5	4	3	2	1

- original text
- collaborative effort
- accurate information
- interesting presentation

Recite a Poem Criteria	5	4	3	2	1

- prepared
- accurate
- speaks clearly
- confident

Respond to a Video Clip Criteria	5	4	3	2	1

- uses "I"
- expresses ideas clearly
- shows insight
- shows connections

Sharefest Criteria	5	4	3	2	1

- participates actively
- is thoughtful
- possesses confidence
- communicates effectively

Song Lyrics Review Criteria	5	4	3	2	1

- convey song's meaning
- show thought and reflection
- give example of poetic device
- use clear language and accurate conventions

Summarize Criteria	5	4	3	2	1

- main idea clearly stated
- only important details in logical sequence
- correct conventions
- specific conclusion

Update Profile Page Criteria	5	4	3	2	1

- engaging voice is evident
- unique
- clear language
- correct conventions

Volunteering Criteria	5	4	3	2	1

- accurate work
- responsible
- shows initiative
- good attitude
- consistent attendance

Lesson Plan Chapter 1
Discovering *My Guide Inside*

Learner Pre-Assessment, then Start with Orientation: Find Your Bearings

*Discovering **My Guide Inside**, inner wisdom, leads to happiness and understanding. Everyone has mental health inside, also defined as a state of well-being. Learning three principles shows how we create our own personal experience of life from the inside-out. Understanding an equation points us to mental well-being and helps us find our bearings:*

"Mind + Consciousness + Thought = Reality." (Banks, 2005, p. 42)

*Exploring the logic of separate realities helps us communicate clearly with others. There's comic relief in seeing separate realities in action! Gaining knowledge of our **Guide Inside** enables us to live a life filled with happiness and well-being. As one teen remarked, "The Three Principles are like your decoder ring!"*

This chapter introduces the Three Principles. These principles are the foundation of MGI. This is the opportunity for students to discover their own Guide Inside that points each student to natural insights and happiness.

Education Learning Objectives and Competencies

With the *MGI* objectives of increasing Personal Well-being Awareness and Responsibility, Chapter 1 begins to prepare students for taking responsibility for their personal well-being and happiness by discussing "Big Picture" ideas, and becoming aware of thoughts. Over time this approach will improve their intellectual, creative, social, emotional, physical and spiritual wellness. There is also a focus on these specific broad competencies: English Language Arts, Communication, Building Healthy Relationships, Social Responsibility, Thinking and Personal Well-being.

Lesson Aims

Chapter 1 aims for learners to:
- begin to understand basic principles of how they operate from the inside out
- listen, collaborate and communicate clearly
- read and view digital resources to explore ideas
- create meaningful texts
- experience creativity

Learning Opportunities
Chapter 1 is designed to encourage learners to:
- gain an understanding of the principles in terms of
  -realizing what they know by reflecting and responding
  -noticing what is happening inside themselves as they learn the principles
- communicate through oral language
- compare ideas with prior knowledge and make connections
- expand knowledge by listening to others and by reading and viewing
- consider others' perspectives and share their own point of view
- create meaningful texts and refine them with enhanced vocabulary
- be creative

Learning Outcomes
At the end of the Chapter 1 lesson, learners will show skills and knowledge through:
- understanding the principles when
  -noticing insights
  -experiencing happiness
- language learning, including vocabulary enhancement in listening and speaking
- applying reading strategies to understand text
- communicating viewpoints to expand thinking
- using clear language and correct conventions in written expression of new ideas from exploring connections to, and reflecting on, "Big Picture" ideas
- expressing creativity

Digital Media Links and Video Clips
Before reading further, please go to the website, myguideinside.com. Once there, look specifically at the links for this chapter. These include: word processing, cloud storage, audio feedback, writing support, image making and banner making tools, as well as video clips. Specifically, these will give you and your students the opportunity to undertake these Digital Media activities: *Reflect and Write a Journal Entry, Respond to a Video Clip, Think of a Time, Create a Work of Art and Create a Banner*. With guidance, these activities will give your students options to share their work with you, the group, the school community and possibly with the global community.

Evaluation Rating Scales for Lesson Activities
Evaluation Rating Scales are provided in this manual for these Chapter 1 activities: journal entries, responses to video clip, writing their thoughts, and creating art and a banner.

Tips for Sharing the Principles
Two resources are helpful in describing what is important to remember when sharing the principles with others. *Guidance for Peer Counselors and Peer Mentors*, for students, is Appendix E of the **MGI Learner Book**. The teacher version, called *Sharing the Principles* is located in Supplemental Resources Section of this Teacher's Manual.

Whenever possible, share your own story including insights and defining moments that impacted your life in a positive way.
Students may also find it interesting to note that we have about 60,000 thoughts per day!

Key Objectives Reminder

Every chapter has two broad learning objectives: Personal Well-being Awareness and Responsibility. With the special focus of Chapter 1, what do the students tell you they have discovered?

Learner self-observation can actually invigorate personal achievement and learning. Most students will grow into seeing the natural outcomes of the lessons as "Usually" apparent in daily life. You can trust that even students who respond in Pre-Assessment as "Rarely" can advance to "Usually." This kind of progress is documented by comparison of student Pre- and Post-Assessments.

End of Chapter 1 Experiment Discussion

Invite students to try the experiment and discuss the results with the group as a segue to Chapter 2. Enjoy!

Lesson Plan Chapter 2
The Lure of Being Secure

Start with Orientation: Find Your Bearings

Everyone wants to feel secure. Insecure feelings can show up in many ways; they wear many different masks. If your head is full of negative thoughts, you will feel insecure. In that state of mind, you experience low moods and in some limited cases even depression. But you are in charge; there is a solution! You have free will to choose which thoughts to pay attention to or "bring to life."

If you are open to it, you can actually see what is going on inside of you. You will learn you are drawn to good feelings and you will actually gravitate to a secure state. When your negative thoughts fall away—when you just let them pass—you will return to a natural feeling of security and enjoy life more. The bonus is you will become grateful and that actually increases your sense of security. One teen explains, "Disguises of insecurity are the masks that we put on when we are feeling uneasy … learning Three Principles has helped me to become more secure about myself and my relationships."

This chapter completes the MGI introduction to the basic foundation of the principles. Students will explore the relationship of Thought, feeling and a secure state of mind, and use intelligence and innate wisdom in communicating their own new viewpoints in relationships with others.

Education Learning Objectives and Competencies

With the *MGI* objectives of increasing Personal Well-being Awareness and Responsibility, Chapter 2 supports students exploring relevance and connection to "Big Picture" ideas such as choosing which thoughts to act on, based on well-being of self and others. Chapter 2 also advances student learning in these broad areas: English Language Arts, Communication, Building Healthy Relationships, Social Responsibility, Self-Determination, Thinking and Personal Well-being.

Lesson Aims: Lee's Story

Chapter 2 aims for learners to:
- gain an understanding of the basic principles of operating from the inside out
- listen, collaborate and communicate clearly
- read and view digital resources to explore ideas
- create meaningful texts
- know to access compassion and be fair
- experience creativity

Learning Opportunities

Chapter 2 is designed to encourage learners to:

- expand an understanding of the principles by
  - -discovering the relationship of thought and feeling
  - -experiencing security when reflecting and relying on their *Guide Inside*
  - -relating to others from this natural intelligence and innate wisdom
- compare ideas with prior knowledge and make connections
- expand knowledge by listening to others, reading and viewing digital resources
- make inferences and consider others' perspectives
- use oral language to expand communication ability
- share their own point of view
- create and refine meaningful texts with enhanced vocabulary
- be creative

Learning Outcomes

At the end of the Chapter 2 lesson, learners will show new skills and knowledge beyond lessons of Chapter 1, including:

- an understanding of the principles when
  - -noticing thoughts and feelings
  - -experiencing security and insecurity
  - -building relationships
- language learning, including vocabulary enhancement in listening and speaking
- applying reading strategies to understand text
- communicating viewpoints to expand thinking
- using clear language and correct conventions in written expression of new ideas from exploring connections to, and reflecting on, "Big Picture" ideas
- expressing creativity

Digital Media Links and Video Clips

Before reading further, please go to the website, myguideinside.com. Once there, look specifically at the links for this chapter. These include: word processing, cloud storage, audio feedback, writing support, presentation tool and video clips. Specifically, these will give you and your students the opportunity to undertake these Digital Media activities: *Reflect and Write a Journal Entry, Respond to a Video Clip, Summarize, and Create a Work of Art*. With guidance, these activities will give your students options to share their work with you, the group, the school community and possibly with the global community.

Evaluation Rating Scales for Lesson Activities

Evaluation Rating Scales are provided in this manual for these Chapter 2 activities: journal entries, responses to video clip, summarizing and creating a work of art.

Key Objectives Reminder

Every chapter has two broad learning objectives: Personal Well-being Awareness and Responsibility. With the special focus of Chapter 2, what do the students tell you they have discovered?

End of Chapter 2 Experiment Discussion

Invite students to try the experiment and discuss the results with the group as a segue to Chapter 3. Enjoy!

BTW: This is an optional clip you may choose to play at your discretion.

"You are not depressed, stop it!" by Prince Ea (Length: 2:26)

Link to clip is provided in teacher resources section of myguideinside.com.

Lesson Plan Chapter 3
Flawsome and Fun: Our True Identity

Start with Orientation: Find Your Bearings
Who and what we are inside is what counts! With one big insight, supermodel Tyra Banks coined the term "flawsome" – awesome even with flaws—when she was publicly criticized for not being physically perfect.

We all have a tendency to hold on to critical thoughts about our identity. We can be our own worst critics. Consider how focusing on faults and judging yourself leads to unhappiness. Have you noticed that when you are contented you are not busy judging yourself or anyone else? Judgment is only a thought; if you allow such personal thinking to pass, you will see with clarity; then it is easy to accept that, like everyone, you are "flawsome." Athletes are also using this knowledge to be "in the zone."

There is logical cause and effect at play: negative thoughts produce negative feelings and positive thoughts create positive feelings. Free will means it's your choice which thoughts receive your attention. There is comic relief in discovering it is all in your head. For example, you may think everyone is watching you but so often, like everyone else, you just perceive an audience. One teen shares: "I experience insights all the time—big and small. I see things closer to how they really are, which is just so cool. It makes you feel so happy and so free. I cherish moments like this, where I really see with no filter. I find moments like [these] to be worth all the craziness."

This chapter deepens understanding of the principles by drawing out learners' inner wisdom and pointing to their true identity. Focus is on the logical cause effect relationship of personal thinking to feeling, and the student's power to choose to hold on to or let go of a thought.

Education Learning Objectives and Competencies
With the *MGI* objectives of increasing Personal Well-being Awareness and Responsibility, Chapter 3 supports students exploring relevance and connection to "Big Picture" ideas such as understanding the cause and effect: thought creates feeling, as well as increasing awareness of thoughts. Chapter 3 also advances student learning in these broad areas: English Language Arts, Communication, Building Healthy Relationships, Social Responsibility, Self-Determination, Thinking and Personal Well-being.

Lesson Aims: Gina's Story
Chapter 3 aims for learners to:
- gain an understanding of basic principles behind their true identity
- listen, collaborate and communicate clearly
- read and view digital resources to explore ideas
- experience creativity and create meaningful texts
- be flexible and resilient
- show perspective and empathy

Learning Opportunities
Chapter 3 is designed to encourage learners to:
- gain an understanding of the principles in terms of
  -the cause and effect relation between personal thinking and feeling
  -the power of choice to drop negative personal thoughts and discover who they really are
  -awareness of personal well-being
- communicate through oral language
- compare ideas with prior knowledge and make connections
- expand knowledge by listening to others and by reading and viewing
- make inferences and consider others' perspectives
- share their own point of view
- create meaningful texts and refine them with enhanced vocabulary
- be creative

Learning Outcomes
At the end of the Chapter 3 lesson, learners will show skills and knowledge through:
- an understanding of the principles to
  -exercise choice about which thoughts to drop or retain
  -relax into the healthy, natural self and personal well-being
- language learning, including vocabulary enhancement in listening and speaking
- applying reading strategies to understand text
- communicating viewpoints to expand thinking
- using clear language and correct conventions in written expression of new ideas from exploring connections to, and reflecting on, "Big Picture" ideas
- expressing creativity

Digital Media Links and Video Clips
Before reading further, please go to the website, myguideinside.com. Once there, look specifically at the links for this chapter. These include: word processing, cloud storage, audio feedback, writing support tool, blogging or website tool, presentation tool and video clips. Specifically, these will give you and your students the opportunity to undertake these Digital Media activities: *Reflect and Write a Journal Entry, Respond to a Video Clip, Create a Listicle, Update*

Profile Page and Create a Work of Art. With guidance, these activities will give your students options to share their work with you, the group, the school community and possibly with the global community.

Evaluation Rating Scales for Lesson Activities
Evaluation Rating Scales are provided in this manual for these Chapter 3 activities: journal entries, responses to video clip, creating a listicle, updating profile page and art.

Key Objectives Reminder
Every chapter has two broad learning objectives: Personal Well-being Awareness and Responsibility. With the special focus of Chapter 3, what do the students tell you they have discovered?

End of Chapter 3 Experiment Discussion Invite students to try the experiment and discuss the results with the group as a segue to Chapter 4. Enjoy!

Lesson Plan Chapter 4
Living in the Present: Leaving the Past in the Dust

Start with Orientation: Find Your Bearings

Many individuals have a rough start in life due to circumstances beyond their control. They may feel confused and angry, thinking they have no other choice. "That is just how life will always be for me." Have you ever been treated with empathy and compassion? What happened?

A caring relationship can open a "chink in the armor" of even the most hardened teens who live with fear and distrust. Just a tiny opening prepares anyone for an insight about the beauty of their true self which is always healthy and undamaged. Those who have lived through hard times and catch this new view of themselves are free and grateful. They find an inner wisdom and inevitably become powerful examples and mentors to others.

*Our **Guide Inside** helps us all see life from a neutral, secure perspective filled with wisdom and joy. A teen says, "We don't have the power to choose the life that we are born into, but we do have the power to create our experience of it. ... Life is a piano. ... You get to write your own music. Your thoughts create your life story. You are the composer. Pick your notes wisely!"*

This chapter stresses that teens have the natural human ability for intuition and insights, which increase personal well-being. Focus is on discovering that difficult circumstances do not determine life experience and that caring relationships may foster life-changing insights in others.

Education Learning Objectives and Competencies

With the *MGI* objectives of increasing Personal Well-being Awareness and Responsibility, Chapter 4 supports students exploring relevance and connection to "Big Picture" ideas such as choosing their *Guide Inside* for impulse control and to regulate behavior effectively. Chapter 4 also advances student learning in these broad areas: English Language Arts, Communication, Building Healthy Relationships, Social Responsibility, Self-Determination and Regulation, Thinking and Personal Well-being.

Lesson Aims: Lenny's Story

Chapter 4 aims for learners to:
- gain an understanding of basic principles behind insights that increase personal well-being
- listen, collaborate and communicate clearly
- read and view digital resources to explore ideas
- create meaningful texts
- motivate themselves and work toward achieving success
- show perspective and empathy

Learning Opportunities

Chapter 4 is designed to encourage learners to:

- gain an understanding of the principles in terms of
  - -realizing everyone has the capacity for insight and intuition despite life circumstances
  - -extending care and empathy to others facing difficulties in life
  - -knowing insights from my *Guide Inside* have the power to change any experience of life
- communicate through oral language
- compare ideas with prior knowledge, discuss language meaning and make connections
- expand knowledge by listening to others and by reading and viewing
- make inferences and consider others' perspectives
- have confidence and show optimism
- be fair and show compassion
- share their own point of view
- create meaningful texts and refine them with enhanced vocabulary
- be creative

Learning Outcomes

At the end of the Chapter 4 lesson, learners will show skills and knowledge through:

- an understanding of the principles when
  - -facing difficult life circumstances
  - -extending a caring relationship to others in distress
- language learning, including vocabulary enhancement in listening and speaking
- applying reading strategies to understand text
- communicating viewpoints to expand thinking
- using clear language and correct conventions in written expression of new ideas from exploring connections to, and reflecting on, "Big Picture" ideas
- expressing creativity

Digital Media Links and Video Clips

Before reading further, please go to the website, myguideinside.com. Once there, look specifically at the links for this chapter. These include: word processing, cloud storage, audio feedback, writing support tool, publishing tool, presentation tool, video sharing tool and video clips. Specifically, these give you and your students the opportunity to undertake these Digital Media activities: *Reflect and Write a Journal Entry, Respond to a Video Clip, Add to the Story, Write a Poem, Create a Work of Art and Recite a Poem.* With guidance, these activities will give your students options to share their work with you, the group, the school community and possibly the global community.

Evaluation Rating Scales for Lesson Activities
Evaluation Rating Scales are provided in this manual for these Chapter 4 activities: journal entry, responses to video clip, adding to the story, writing a poem, creating art and reciting a poem.

Key Objectives Reminder
Every chapter has two broad learning objectives: Personal Well-being Awareness and Responsibility. With the special focus of Chapter 4, what do the students tell you they have discovered?

End of Chapter 4 Experiment Discussion
Invite students to try the experiment and discuss the results with the group as a segue to Chapter 5. Enjoy!

Lesson Plan Chapter 5
Understanding the Lost Thinker

Start with Orientation: Find Your Bearings

We all have been lost thinkers at times. Sometimes we act like aggressors and in other situations we feel like victims. There is actually only one problem. Everyone occasionally pays attention to misleading thoughts. You may think you or a friend feels social pressures to be a certain way or do something. The solution is to listen to your **Guide Inside**, *innate inner wisdom, to gain a more accurate understanding.*

You are part of several groups or mini-cultures. Not every group member may be directly part of a social problem but everyone can be part of the solution. You may not personally be dealing with a difficulty but you may clearly notice that someone else is. Your wisdom can help you understand how to support peers who face challenges. No one needs to live in the shadows. You can have insights about how to treat someone with encouragement, kindness and dignity. A little support goes a long, long way.

As one teen reflects, "When we relate from a place of caring and understanding instead of anger and retaliation, we give others the opportunity to let go of the negative thought patterns creating their unpleasant lives. This naturally creates a more easy-going world for everyone."

This chapter creates opportunities for students to see themselves occasionally as "lost thinkers" and use common sense and reflection to experience new thinking. This improves communication skills and increases social and digital responsibility.

Education Learning Objectives and Competencies

With the *MGI* objectives of increasing Personal Well-being Awareness and Responsibility, Chapter 5 supports students exploring relevance and connection to "Big Picture" ideas such as choosing which thoughts to pay attention to and identifying healthy thoughts and feelings. Chapter 5 also advances student learning in these broad areas: English Language Arts, Communication, Building Healthy Relationships, Social Responsibility, Positive Personal and Cultural Identity, Self-Determination and Regulation, Thinking and Personal Well-being.

Lesson Aims: Sarah and Ruby's Story

Chapter 5 aims for learners to:
- gain an understanding of basic principles behind getting "lost in thought"
- listen, collaborate and communicate clearly
- read and view digital resources to explore ideas
- expand communication and create meaningful texts

- have confidence and advocate for themselves
- respond suitably to discrimination and harassment
- access knowledge to support healthy decisions and understand personal safety
- show perspective and empathy
- show inclusive actions and contribute to the community

Learning Opportunities

Chapter 5 is designed to encourage learners to:
- gain an understanding of the principles in terms of
  -realizing what they know by reflecting and responding with common sense
  -finding new ideas, insights, leading to healthy thinking and feeling, which naturally leads to responsible behavior
- compare ideas with prior knowledge, discuss language meaning and make connections
- communicate through oral language
- expand knowledge by listening to others and by reading and viewing
- make inferences and consider others' perspectives
- share their own point of view
- create meaningful texts and refine them with enhanced vocabulary
- be creative

Learning Outcomes

At the end of the Chapter 5 lesson, learners will show skills and knowledge through:
- an understanding of the principles to
  -regain well-being with reflection by listening to my *Guide Inside*
  -use common sense to act responsibly in social and digital relationships
- language learning, including vocabulary enhancement in listening and speaking
- applying reading strategies to understand text
- communicating viewpoints to expand thinking
- using clear language and correct conventions in written expression of new ideas from exploring connections to, and reflecting on, "Big Picture" ideas
- expressing creativity

Digital Media Links and Video Clips

Before reading further, please go to the website, myguideinside.com. Once there, look specifically at the links for this chapter. These include: word processing, cloud storage, audio feedback, file sharing tool, writing support tool, blogging tool, image making tool and video clips. Specifically, these will give you and your students the opportunity to undertake these Digital Media activities: *Reflect and Write a Journal Entry, Respond to a Video Clip, Create a Public Service Announcement, Create a Blog and Create a Poster*. With guidance, these activities will give your students options to share their work with you, the group, the school community and possibly the global community.

Evaluation Rating Scales for Lesson Activities

Evaluation Rating Scales are provided in this manual for these Chapter 5 activities: journal entry, responses to video clip, public service announcement, blogging and a poster.

Key Objectives Reminder

Every chapter has two broad learning objectives: Personal Well-being Awareness and Responsibility. With the special focus of Chapter 5, what do the students tell you they have discovered?

End of Chapter 5 Experiment Discussion

Invite students to try the experiment and discuss the results with the group as a segue to Chapter 6. Enjoy!

BTW: This is an optional clip you may choose to play at your discretion.
"Dear angry Facebook user, this is for you," by Prince Ea (Length 4:01)
Link to clip is provided in teacher resources section of myguideinside.com.

Lesson Plan Chapter 6
Making Room for Happiness

Start with Orientation: Find Your Bearings

You can get rid of negative thoughts that stop you from living in the present. You have free will to navigate life moment-to-moment. An insight can happen anytime; however, a calm state of mind naturally produces helpful insights. With inner wisdom as your guide, you will experience happiness.

Did you know the past is only a thought you choose to carry through time? The past is your own memory. You rather naturally decide what you do with it. As you begin to learn the logic of how your own experience—reality—is created, you will notice a change in yourself. Your memories begin to shift and change as you have new insights. In this way you get a deeper, richer understanding of life. And the biggest surprise of all is that you will discover you actually have healthier feelings for yourself and also for others. The really good news is your understanding of this inside-out nature just keeps growing.

As one teen writes, "We are learning to not allow our negative thoughts to control us. We can open our heart and change to positive thoughts."

In this chapter, students use inner intelligence to gain a healthy perspective on past experiences. Focus is on the logic of how personal experience is created by a student's own thinking. As a result, in a calm state of mind, students discover healthy thoughts and feelings about themselves and others, and communicate their ideas effectively.

Education Learning Objectives and Competencies

With the *MGI* objectives of increasing Personal Well-being Awareness and Responsibility, Chapter 6 supports students exploring relevance and connection to "Big Picture" ideas such as letting new thought emerge. Chapter 6 also advances student learning in these broad areas: English Language Arts, Communication, Building Healthy Relationships, Social Responsibility, Self-Determination and Regulation, Thinking and Personal Well-being.

Lesson Aims: Kailani's and Lilianna's Stories

Chapter 6 aims for learners to:
- gain an understanding of basic principles leading to a healthy perspective on the past
- listen, collaborate and communicate clearly
- read and view digital resources to explore ideas
- expand communication and create meaningful texts

- be fair, show perspective and empathy
- show optimism

Learning Opportunities

Chapter 6 is designed to encourage learners to:
- gain an understanding of the principles in terms of
  -discovering the logic of how personal experience is created by personal thinking
  -experiencing the benefits of a calm state of mind leading to new perspectives
- compare ideas with prior knowledge and make connections
- communicate through oral language
- expand knowledge by listening to others and by reading and viewing
- make inferences and consider others' perspectives
- share their own point of view
- create meaningful texts and refine them with enhanced vocabulary
- synthesize texts to create insight
- be creative

Learning Outcomes

At the end of the Chapter 6 lesson, learners will show skills and knowledge through:
- an understanding of the principles when
  -listening to my *Guide Inside* while reflecting on past experiences
  -experiencing new insights and clarity
  -enjoying life and relationships from this new vantage point
- language learning, including vocabulary enhancement in listening and speaking
- applying reading strategies to understand text
- communicating viewpoints to expand thinking
- using clear language and correct conventions in written expression of new ideas from exploring connections to, and reflecting on, "Big Picture" ideas
- expressing creativity

Digital Media Links and Video Clips

Before reading further, please go to the website, myguideinside.com. Once there, look specifically at the links for this chapter. These include: word processing, cloud storage, audio feedback, image making tool, note taking tool, writing support tool, podcasting tool, presentation tool and video clips. Specifically, these will give you and your students the opportunity to undertake these Digital Media activities: *Reflect and Write a Journal Entry, Respond to a Video Clip, Persuasive Writing, Fast Forward Profiling, Volunteering and Song Lyrics Review*. With guidance, these activities will give your students options to share their work with you, the group, the school community and possibly the global community.

Evaluation Rating Scales for Lesson Activities

Evaluation Rating Scales are provided in this manual for these Chapter 6 activities: journal entry, responses to video clip, persuasive writing, fast forward profiling, volunteering and song lyrics review.

Key Objectives Reminder
Every chapter has two broad learning objectives: Personal Well-being Awareness and Responsibility. With the special focus of Chapter 6, what do the students tell you they have discovered?

End of Chapter 6 Experiment Discussion
Invite students to try the experiment and discuss the results with the group as a segue to Chapter 7. Enjoy!

Lesson Plan Chapter 7
Facing the Future in a State of Well-being

Start with Orientation: Find Your Bearings

You can look to the future with hope. It is true. Inner wisdom is always available and you will see that worry, anxiety and overwhelm are needless thoughts that distract you from success. There's no common sense in using your thoughts against yourself! Happiness, well-being and a feeling of security go hand in hand. Your own good attitude is an outcome of understanding the logic of the Three Principles.

As one teen advises, "It's like a sugar pill, if you think that you'll feel insecure, then you will. Get past that, then you're as good as golden, 'cause beyond that it's just physical ability to get work done. Just think about everyone else who's gone through this same obstacle and who's succeeded, they're not much different from who you are."

In this chapter, learners find hope, happiness and well-being. Focus is on discovering that learning the Three Principles Equation has the natural outcome of a good attitude. Worry, anxiety and overwhelm become needless and distracting.

Education Learning Objectives and Competencies

With the *MGI* objectives of increasing Personal Well-being Awareness and Responsibility, Chapter 7 supports students taking increasing responsibility for their personal well-being, happiness and success. Chapter 7 also advances student learning in these broad areas: English Language Arts, Communication, Building Healthy Relationships, Personal Responsibility, Self-Determination and Regulation, Thinking and Personal Well-being.

Lesson Aims: Byron's Story

Chapter 7 aims for learners to:
- gain an understanding of basic principles leading to happiness and personal well-being
- listen, collaborate and communicate clearly
- read and view digital resources to explore ideas
- expand communication and create meaningful texts
- be flexible and resilient
- have confidence and an awareness of strengths
- show optimism; a good attitude

Learning Opportunities

Chapter 7 is designed to encourage learners to:
- gain an understanding of the principles by
  - learning the Three Principles Equation
  - discovering a good attitude is a natural outcome of living from these principles
- compare ideas with prior knowledge and make connections
- communicate through oral language
- expand knowledge by listening to others and by reading and viewing
- make inferences and consider others' perspectives
- share their own point of view
- create meaningful texts and refine them with enhanced vocabulary
- synthesize texts to create insight
- be creative

Learning Outcomes

At the end of the Chapter 7 lesson, learners will show skills and knowledge through:
- an understanding of the principles when
  - being free of anxiety, worry, and overwhelm
  - enjoying a good attitude
  - experiencing hope
- language learning, including vocabulary enhancement in listening and speaking
- applying reading strategies to understand text
- communicating viewpoints to expand thinking
- using clear language and correct conventions in written expression of new ideas from exploring connections to, and reflecting on, "Big Picture" ideas
- expressing creativity

Digital Media Links and Video Clips

Before reading further, please go to the website, myguideinside.com. Once there, look specifically at the links for this chapter. These include: word processing, cloud storage, audio feedback, podcasting tool and video clips. Specifically, these will give you and your students the opportunity to undertake these Digital Media activities: *Reflect and Write a Journal Entry, Respond to a Video Clip, Sharefest, Interview Report and Create a Dream Theme*. With guidance, these activities will give your students options to share their work with you, the group, the school community and possibly the global community.

Evaluation Rating Scales for Lesson Activities

Evaluation Rating Scales are provided in this manual for these Chapter 7 activities: journal entry, responses to video clip, sharefest, interview report and creating a dream theme.

Key Objectives Reminder

Every chapter has two broad learning objectives: Personal Well-being Awareness and Responsibility. With the special focus of Chapter 7, what do the students tell you they have discovered?

End of Chapter 7 Experiment Discussion

Invite students to try the experiment and discuss the results of the experiment with the group as a segue to Chapter 8. Enjoy!

Lesson Plan Chapter 8
Defining Your Individual Path

Start with Orientation: Find Your Bearings

Congratulations! You are ready to review your most important lessons to be prepared for the best life possible. Remember what you already know:

*Your **Guide Inside** is natural inner wisdom. Happiness is a state of mind, and separate realities mean we each see the world in our own unique way. You will experience more security if you let go of insecure thoughts. Moods are simply caused by the thoughts you hold on to. Moods naturally fluctuate as your thinking shifts and flows.*

Stop paying attention to distressful or contaminated thinking, and you end up "in the zone" more of the time. Furthermore, the past is past. Because the past is tied to your thinking, paying attention to your insights guides you to natural wisdom and joy. Be gentle on yourself and others when the "lost thinker" temporarily seems real. Remember, when you are calm, it is easier to notice insights and drop unhelpful thinking. A new perspective will always show up. No matter what, worry is useless and a calm state of mind naturally produces a good attitude.

In this final chapter, learners are invited to synthesize their learning and realize this growth occurs lifelong. This chapter focuses on remembering what they have learned as they go forward in life. Students are encouraged take advantage of wonderful multi-media activities. This final session asks them to create, share and enjoy what they understand about their Guide Inside.

Education Learning Objectives and Competencies

With the *MGI* objectives of increasing Personal Well-being Awareness and Responsibility, this final chapter also advances student learning in these broad areas: English Language Arts, Communication, Building Healthy Relationships, Social Responsibility, Positive Personal and Cultural Identity, Self-Determination and Regulation, Thinking and Personal Well-being.

Lesson Aims

Chapter 8 aims for learners to:
- synthesize an understanding of the principles including, but not limited, to:
  - the importance of letting new thought emerge
  - seeing that inner wisdom—their *Guide Inside*—can help them navigate life (24/7/365)
  - becoming increasingly aware of thoughts and actions naturally increases personal well-being and responsibility

- listen, collaborate and communicate clearly
- read and view to explore ideas
- expand communication and create meaningful texts
- have confidence and an awareness of strengths
- understand their positive identity can be symbolized as a metaphor
- understand their identity evolves as they gain understanding of the power of Thought
- identify people who can support them as well as see that they can also give help
- monitor own progress

Learning Opportunities

Chapter 8 is designed to encourage learners to:

- live from an understanding of the principles in order to:
  - experience happiness, academic success and healthy relationships
  - follow their *Guide Inside* to access new ideas, insights, that enhance life
- compare ideas with prior knowledge and make connections
- communicate through oral language
- expand knowledge by listening to others and by reading and viewing
- make inferences and consider others' perspectives
- share their own point of view
- create meaningful texts and refine them with enhanced vocabulary
- synthesize texts to create insight
- be creative

Learning Outcomes

At the end of the Chapter 8 lesson, learners will show skills and knowledge through:

- showing confidence in an understanding of the principles to:
  - support personal well-being
  - enable healthy relationships with others
  - realize optimal social and digital responsibility
  - communicate meaningfully and effectively
  - maximize personal health and quality of life
- language learning, including vocabulary enhancement in listening and speaking
- applying reading strategies to understand text
- communicating viewpoints to expand thinking
- using clear language and correct conventions in written expression of new ideas from exploring connections to, and reflecting on, "Big Picture" ideas
- expressing creativity
- reflecting on Chapter 8 "Reminders" in Appendix D
- assessing progress with Learner Post-assessment

Digital Media Links

Before reading further, please go to the website, myguideinside.com. Once there, look specifically at the links for this chapter. These include: word processing, cloud storage, audio feedback, mind mapping tool and video production tool. Specifically, these will give you and your students the opportunity to undertake these Digital Media activities: *Reflect and Write a Journal Entry, Create a Belonging Map and a Personal Metaphor*. With guidance, these activities will give your students options to share their work with you, the group, the school community and possibly the global community.

Evaluation Rating Scales for Lesson Activities

Evaluation Rating Scales are provided in this manual for these Chapter 8 activities: journal entry, belonging map and personal metaphor.

Final Class Assessments

Instruct learners to complete the Learner Post-assessment. Have them compare their Pre- and Post- Assessments and discuss the sense of progress. They could do this privately with you or with the class as appropriate. The assessments allow students and teacher to monitor personal progress.

Complete Teacher *"Snapshot" Observations MGI III* on each learner at the end of the final class. The final class comparisons of the "Snapshot" are important to share with your school administrators and policy makers. These questions are common concerns and growth in these areas influences *MGI* use in the future or when to refer a specific student into this class/ learning. Give individual students, as well as the class as a whole, feedback—authentic evidence of their gains in awareness and understanding that you observe.

Conclude with a celebration.

Final Note to Teachers

When you have completed this class do take time to reflect on what you have done well and what you might try in the future. Especially pay attention to what your own wisdom reveals about your teaching experience with *My Guide Inside*. How has it impacted not only your students, but you yourself? Sydney Banks advises us to *exercise our choice and find inner wisdom for ourselves*. Once found, we naturally share and we are advised by John Hattie to know our impact. Now that's simple logic.

Congratulations on making a difference in the world!

❖ *My Guide Inside* **Meets Educational Learning Objectives, Competencies**

Current Education Policy Context:
Undoubtedly, as an educator you are responsible for meeting official learning objectives and student competency standards. *My Guide Inside* is designed to help you do that.

As we write this *Teacher's Manual*, the British Columbia Ministry of Education in Canada is developing a new curriculum including, *"Personal Awareness and Responsibility Competence Profile."*

The most current version of that work states, "Personal awareness and responsibility is one of the three interrelated competencies that relate to the broad area of Social and Emotional Learning." The curriculum further explains Personal Awareness and Responsibility competency involves: Self-determination, Self-regulation, and Well-being. The Ministry discusses Well-being this way:

> *"Students who are personally aware and responsible recognize how their decisions and actions affect their mental, physical, emotional, social, cognitive, and spiritual wellness, and take increasing responsibility for caring for themselves. They keep themselves healthy and physically active, manage stress, and express a sense of personal well-being. … They recognize the importance of happiness, and have strategies that help them find peace in challenging situations."*
> (Personal Awareness and Responsibility Competence Profiles, p. 3)

There is also an interest in promoting well-being in the United Kingdom's schools. According to "Promoting Fundamental British Values as part of SMSC in Schools," schools must "promote the spiritual, moral, social and cultural (SMSC) development of their pupils." At this time there is increasing awareness globally of the need for all education systems to support and foster lifelong well-being of students. In that sense this comprehensive Pre-K-12 *My Guide Inside* curriculum is a timely resource for all educators and their school systems.

Regardless of where you are located in the world, this material is suited for and meets selected requirements for English Language Arts (ELA), Health Education, Career Education, and Personal, Social, Health & Economic Education (PSHE). It supports inclusion and may be used to develop competencies in Communication (C), Thinking (T) and Social and Emotional Learning (SEL), which includes decision making, self-management, healthy relationships and well-being. It also may be used to develop competencies in Personal & Social Responsibility (PS), which includes positive personal and cultural identity, personal awareness and responsibility, spiritual wellness, as well as social responsibility.

Learners everywhere can discover my *Guide Inside*, also referred simply as common sense or wisdom. They become increasingly aware of and take responsibility for thoughts and actions that impact their intellectual, creative, social, emotional and physical potentials as well as their spiritual wellness. Accessing natural inner wisdom produces joy, love, compassion, personal strength, and leads to academic success. The principles on which this curriculum is based are the key to innate mental health characterized by optimism, resilience, and well-being.

Understanding these principles actually supports and increases a student's well-being, self-efficacy and self-confidence; and improves ability to self-regulate, set goals, and take responsibilities for their choices and actions. With understanding, students become patient learning over time, persevere in difficult situations to solve problems calmly, and realize the logic of how their actions affect themselves and others.

Objectives of *My Guide Inside*

The principles operate in all people, including every teen. This *MGI* curriculum points the way to wholeness, happiness, creativity and well-being in all parts of life.

Therefore, MGI **has these two academic goals: (1) to enhance Personal Well-being with an understanding of these principles,** and **(2) to develop competencies in Communication, Thinking, and Personal and Social Responsibility.** *MGI* accomplishes both goals by using stories, discussion and various written and creative activities, as it increases competency in English Language Arts, including Digital Media.

Discovering our *Guide Inside*, key to learning, enhances ability to make decisions, navigate life and build healthy relationships. Accessing that natural wisdom will affect well-being, spiritual wellness, personal and social responsibility, and positive personal and cultural identity. We start by uploading happiness.

Please consider how the MGI curriculum also meets these requirements common to most school systems globally:

Educational Learning Objectives and Competencies:

- **English Language Arts Competencies**
  Reading and Viewing: Learners will expand their knowledge and apply strategies to understand, compare ideas with prior knowledge, make inferences, reflect, and respond. Learners will enhance their vocabulary while they read and view for enjoyment, to explore ideas and to inspire creativity. They will synthesize texts to create insight and communicate viewpoints to expand thinking.

  Writing and Representation: Learners will expand their communication and create meaningful texts, including visual texts, that show depth of thought and have a logical sequence. Learners will refine texts with enhanced vocabulary, clear language and correct conventions of grammar, spelling and punctuation. Learners will use an engaging "voice" and present texts in a variety of ways.

Oral Language: Listening and speaking are foundations of language learning for developing vocabulary, making connections and having perspective. Learners will expand knowledge by listening to others as well as realizing what they themselves know by reflecting, expressing their own point of view and communicating through oral language. Learners will rehearse and perform to produce language and discuss language meaning.

- **Communication Competency**
Learners will share with others in conversation to develop understanding and relationships. Learners will collaborate on activities, including effective use of Digital Media, to present their work. Students will acquire knowledge and share what they have learned through presentations, self-monitoring and self-assessment.

- **Health Education, Career Education, and Personal, Social, Health & Economic Education Objectives**
Learners will respond suitably to discrimination and harassment, show respect and understand what makes and maintains a healthy relationship. Learners will identify supportive relationships, healthy thoughts and feelings, and understand personal safety. Learners will access knowledge to support healthy decisions.

- **Personal & Social Competencies (Social Emotional Learning)**
Personal Responsibility: Learners can anticipate results of own actions. They understand and become increasingly aware of and take responsibility for thoughts and actions that impact their intellectual, creative, social, emotional and physical potentials, as well as their spiritual wellness. They are flexible; making responsible decisions about which thoughts to act on, based on well-being of self and others.
  – **Well-being**: Through an understanding of my *Guide Inside*, ever-present natural inner wisdom or common sense, learners take increasing responsibility for their personal well-being, which includes their safety and happiness. Learners understand that mental health is a state of well-being.
  – **Self-Determination**: Learners understand the cause and effect rule that thought creates feeling and thought is the "seed" of behavior. Learners have confidence, an awareness of strengths to face challenges and know to access compassion. Learners advocate for themselves.
  – **Self-Regulation**: Learners choose their *Guide Inside* (their own natural inner wisdom) to regulate behavior effectively and control impulses. Learners show honesty, motivate themselves and work toward achieving success.

Social Responsibility: Learners are fair, appreciate others' perspectives and solve problems in peaceful ways. They show empathy, compassion and understanding, and are inclusive and contribute to the community.

  – **Healthy Relationships**: Learners listen, co-operate and communicate clearly. They show compassion, empathy and understanding, solve people problems calmly, and seek and offer help when needed.

  – **Positive Personal and Cultural Identity**: Learners understand their identity evolves as they gain understanding and experience in life. Learners see that natural inner wisdom combined with personal attributes can help them navigate life. Learners identify people who can support them as well as see that they can also offer help.

- **Thinking Competency**

  Learners will gain awareness of the power of Thought, which is the thinking process in action. They will generate creative ideas while investigating relevance and con- nection to "Big Picture" ideas. They will learn that their ideas have value. Learners will understand to let the personal mind clear to allow new thought to emerge. They will have opportunities to develop new ideas, insights, that change what they do in life. Learners will choose which thoughts to pay attention to, which logically lead to intended outcomes.

❖ **Understanding Teens Today**

One additional element of successful student achievement and effective teaching is so obvious it can often be overlooked. The degree to which both students and educators understand the real lives of teens today matters.

Just as Dr. Pettit stated, there is tremendous value in educating teens about their *Guide Inside* so that they overcome mental awkwardness. Students truly can come to understand and navi- gate life smoothly as they mature from childhood to adult life.

The teen years are characterized by both innocence and worldliness. Teens are living a paradox. We can accompany and support them as they create identity, realize well-being, discover purpose and learn who and what they are. As daunting as it may seem, we educators are prepared for this task. It is made easier in that teens are surprisingly astute when it comes to adults being present and authentic with them—they so appreciate it! Their keen awareness empowers them to offer insights and helpful perspectives to the adults they are secure with.

We have had our own teen times—being a teen, living with and raising teens, studying teen development, educating teens and having ordinary conversations with teens. In this process we have all come to understand many truths:

Teens looking for Identity are often prone to:
- be eager to investigate. "Who and what am I, really?"
- be creative, curious and lighthearted
- observe flaws in others, yet sensitive and vulnerable about their own flaws
- clutch mental ups and downs, yet see moods shift swiftly
- want respect for uniqueness, yet feel isolated because of uniqueness
- want direction, yet also want independence
- experience hope for the future

Teens in relationships often:
- are interested in talking about their lives with adults
- care about equality, yet may be inconsiderate of others
- are occupied with being the center, yet feel a need to be connected to others
- perceive an audience, yet don't notice others (Berk, 2007.)
- need a healthy relationship with a significant adult, yet won't always accept advice
- feel misunderstood by adults, yet need reinforcement that adults care
- see peers as important, yet depend on parental values
- want adult mentors, yet can become rebellious and test limits
- develop independence, yet still need reassurance that significant adults care
- are open to adult influence

Teens can benefit from:
- time alone to reflect on the day
- variety of activity, rest and change
- feeling safe, nurtured and valued
- practice making healthy decisions
- seeking healthy adventures and taking positive risks
- time for plenty of sleep
- invitation to think about ideas
- clarifying own thinking through conversing
- spiritual wellness gained by discussing the "Big Picture" of life

❖ *MGI* **Learning Opportunities Designed for Teens**

All *MGI* lessons and activities are designed to accommodate these characteristics of teens. Therefore, *MGI* specifically includes opportunities for teens to:
- make connections with what they are learning
- write reflective journal entry daily
- receive feedback when they share their thoughts
- exercise personal choice from a variety of options
- discover new interests
- seek out healthy risk-taking by stretching boundaries
- be active (including outdoors) and interactive when learning
- discover the logic of cause and effect
- start understanding abstractions and metaphors
- think independently
- clarify own thinking
- expand understanding through: Think, Pair, Share
- develop relationships and sense of connection
- monitor own understanding
- accept support with making healthy decisions
- find relevance in solving real-life problems
- collaborate on activities
- be creative with language activities
- improve academic performance
- engage in storytelling
- be lighthearted and see humor
- play games
- create their identity
- experience compassion and joy in life
- enhance their well-being and spiritual wellness
- satisfy their thirst for knowledge of natural inner wisdom or *Guide Inside*

References Cited

Aust, B. (2016). Field notes: Capturing the moment with a story. *ASCD Express*. Retrieved from www.ascd.org/ascd-express/vol12/1207-aust.aspx

Aust, B. (2013). *The Essential Curriculum: 21 iIdeas for Developing a Positive and Optimistic Culture*. North Charleston: CreateSpace Independent Publishing Platform.

Banks, S. (1998). *The Missing Link: Reflections on Philosophy & Spirit*. Edmonton: International Human Relations Consultants.

Banks, S. (2005). *Enlightened Gardener Revisited*. Edmonton: International Human Relations Consultants.

Berk, L. (2007). *Development through the lifespan*. Boston: Allyn and Bacon.

Campsall, C. and J. Tucker. 2016. *My Guide Inside: (Book II) Knowing Myself and Understanding my world: Rated: E for everyone*. North Charleston: CreateSpace Independent Publishing Platform.

Donohoo, J. (2016). *Collective efficacy: How educators' beliefs impact student learning*. Thousand Oaks: Corwin Press.

Hattie, J. "The Applicability of Visible Learning to Higher Education." *Scholarship of Teaching and Learning in Psychology* 1.1 (2015): 79-91. Retrieved from http://www.dx.doi.org.ezp3.lib.umn.edu/10.1037/stl0000021

"Hattie Ranking - Interactive Visualization." *Hattie Ranking: Interactive Visualization - VISIBLE LEARNING*, visible-learning.org. Retrieved from http://www.nvd3/visualize/hattie-ranking-interactive-2009-2011-2015

"Personal Awareness and Responsibility Competence Profiles." (2016). *BC's New Curriculum*. Retrieved from http://www.curriculum.gov.bc.ca/competencies/personal-awareness-responsibility

"Personal, Social, Health and Economic (PSHE) Education." *Gov.UK*. Retrieved from http://www.gov.uk

"Promoting Fundamental British Values as part of SMSC in Schools" (2014). *Gov.UK*. Retrieved from http://www.gov.uk

"Sharing the Principles of Mind, Consciousness, and Thought by Elsie Spittle and George Pransky in Collaboration with Three Principle Practitioners - 3PGC Blog." 3PGC. Retrieved from http://www.3pgc.org

"Year-Long Series - Educators Living in the Joy of Gratitude." (2016). *3 Principles Supermind*. Retrieved from http://www.threeprinciplessupermind.com/products/educators-living-the-joy-of-gratitude.254

Sharing the Principles of Mind, Consciousness, and Thought
by
Elsie Spittle and Dr. George Pransky
in
Collaboration with Three Principle Practitioners
(Adapted with permission for teachers, counselors, and youth mentors)

Based on the direct teachings of Sydney Banks, the purpose of this document is to offer what we learned from Sydney Banks about how to effectively share our understanding of the Three Principles. This document is not about the Principles themselves, but exclusively about guidance for sharing the Principles. Here are the key points Syd would point us toward:

1. Health of the helper:
   What ultimately qualifies a teacher is the extent to which that person reflects and demonstrates the quality of life that learners desire (we call it "grounding"), and the teacher's ability to share what he or she understands that accounts for that quality of life.
2. Look to your student's innate mental health, not what's wrong:
   There is a wisdom and logic to the Principles that exists in all living things.
3. Insight/pure intelligence:
   The realization of innate wisdom or pure intelligence comes from within the listener via insight. Every learner has innate wisdom within him/her.
4. Deepening levels of consciousness:
   Learning and understanding the Principles is a matter of the heart and not of the intellect. True understanding will bypass the intellect. We have learned to keep the message simple rather than analytical and complicated.
5. A friendly conversation:
   There is a great value in leveling the playing field and talking with your students much as you would in a friendly conversation. What would traditionally be called "teaching" shifts more to drawing wisdom out from learners and has the feeling of "sharing."
6. Listening to truth:
   We learned from Syd that the truth of the Principles can only be seen via insight. No manner of trying to figure things out ever really helped. Insight is not limited by anything. It can happen at any time from any state of mind. That said, however, a quiet, reflective mind is a more conducive medium for insight rather than an active, analytical listening process.
7. Listening to your students:
   We learned to listen beyond the youth's story to hear their wisdom, and to point them in that direction. This will help youth see that they know what to do, no matter what their history has been, or what has happened to them.
8. Stick to what you know:
   It is important that we stick with what we know (what is real for us) and not try to talk beyond our grounding. When we share only what we know, we will see more. What we

know now is more than enough for now. Syd often said that "what little we know might be decades ahead of its time."

9. Sharing our story:

    Some things don't lend themselves to direct, easy expression. The Principles fall into that category. Stories and metaphors can be helpful in this regard. Syd also encouraged us to share our own personal story—to the degree that is appropriate with our students — (how we came to understand the Principles and what we saw for ourselves). We learned that sharing our story brings our understanding of the Principles to life. It is the deep feeling of well-being that occurs when we share our story that helps awaken the innate mental health in those with whom we are speaking. Our story will also point to the results produced by our usage of the Principles and provide hope.

10. Connecting the dots:

    When learners have insights, they change. They see and hear differently and feel different, but they may not always realize this at first. Pointing this out in the context of our students' results has great value. It releases a feeling of hope. The feeling the learner is experiencing is more informative to the teacher than the young person's grasp of the content.

11. Stick to the Principles:

    Syd reminded us that everyone has the wisdom and understanding within themselves to stabilize and solve their problems. Practitioner techniques intended to "improve student wellbeing" disempower youths, because it undermines the message that they have all they need within themselves. The Principles empower students by pointing them to their own wisdom, creativity and natural resilience.

12. Trust your inner wisdom/pure intelligence:

    Ultimately, we all want to trust and follow our own wisdom, what we personally understand. That said, we also want to be open to hearing/seeing more than we do right now. This means listening from within, and being open to hearing something new; something that will deepen our grounding and growth. Syd expressed that point eloquently by saying: "Don't be a follower; a listener, yes, but not a follower."

13. Have your heart in the right place:

    Not long after Sydney Banks had his profound experience, he knew that what he had realized would be of great help to humanity. He set his sights on being of service and encouraged those who learned from him to point in that direction as well. In service, we will find our teaching more fulfilling and impactful. We have seen time and again that when our priority is being in service to humanity and being true to our own wisdom, the practical aspects of life inevitably fall into place; often in ways we couldn't possibly have imagined.

For full document see: https://goo.gl/OIxcsp. (Accessed 22 Oct. 2016).

Recommended Three Principles Resources

By Sydney Banks:
Books
Second Chance (1983)
In Quest of the Pearl (1989)
The Missing Link: Reflections on Philosophy and Spirit (1998)
The Enlightened Gardener (2001)
Dear Liza (2004)
The Enlightened Gardener Revisited (2005)

CDs

Attitude!	*In Quest of the Pearl*	*Second Chance*
Great Spirit, The	*Long Beach Lectures*	*Washington Lectures*
Hawaii Lectures	*One Thought Away*	*What is Truth*

DVDs

Hawaii Lectures (1-4)	*Washington Lectures (1-2)*
Long Beach Lectures (1-4)	*The Ultimate Answer*

Books, CDs and DVDs are available through:
sydbanks.com, amazon.com or
Lone Pine Publishing: 1-800-518-3541 (US) 1-800 875 7108 (Canada)
Available in the UK and Europe from SydneyBanksProducts.com.

Continued Learning for Educators

The Power of the Three Principles in Schools Four-part free online professional development series for educators created by Christa Campsall and Barb Aust. This series links to Sydney Banks Long Beach Lectures
www.ed-talks.com/resources

Long Beach Lectures (1-4) video series of presentations by Sydney Banks
www.sydbanks.com/longbeach/

Educators Living in the Joy of Gratitude (18 free recorded professional development programs facilitated by Kathy Marshall Emerson. These feature Barb Aust, Christa Campsall, and many other seasoned educators sharing the principles globally. Includes MGI curriculum orientation and official student focus group.)
www.nationalresilienceresource.com/Educator-Preparation.html

Education and Three Principles Christa and Bob Campsall video presentation
www.3pgc.org/photos-videos/details/?m=1185

Seeing Beyond Behavior in Youth Webinar with Christa Campsall
https://vimeo.com/157500313

Selected Principles Publications for Educators

Aust, B. (2016). Field notes: Capturing the moment with a story. *ASCD Express*. Retrieved from www.ascd.org/ascd-express/vol12/1207-aust.aspx

Aust, B. (2013). *The Essential Curriculum: 21 Ideas for Developing a Positive and Optimistic Culture*. Author.

Aust, B., & Vine, W. (2003, October). The power of voice in schools. *ASCD Classroom Leadrship*, 7, 5, 8.

Campsall, C. (2005). Increasing student sense of feeling safe: The role of thought and common sense in developing social responsibility. Unpublished master's thesis. Royal Roads University, Victoria, British Columbia, Canada.

Marshall Emerson, K. (2015). "Resilience research and community practice: A view from the bridge." Paper presented to the Pathways to Resilience III, 6/19/2015, Halifax, Nova Scotia.

Marshall, K. (2005, September). Resilience in our schools: Discovering mental health and hope from the inside-out. In D. L. White, M. K. Faber, & B. C. Glenn (Eds.). *Proceedings of Persistently Safe Schools 2005*. 128-140. Washington, DC: Hamilton Fish Institute, The George Washington University for U. S. Department of Justice, Office of Juvenile Justice and Delinquency Prevention.

Marshall, K. (2004). Resilience research and practice: National Resilience Resource Center bridging the gap. In H. C. Waxman, Y. N. Padron and J. Gray (Eds.). *Educational resiliency: student, teacher, and school perspectives*. Pp. 63-84. Greenwich, CT: Information Age Publishing.

Marshall, K. (November, 1998). Reculturing systems with resilience/health realization. *Promoting positive and healthy behaviors in children: Fourteenth annual Rosalynn Carter symposium on mental health Policy*. Atlanta, GA: The Carter Center, pp. 48-58.

Websites
3 Principles Ed Talks: www.ed-talks.com.
National Resilience Resource Center: www.nationalresilienceresource.com.
Sydney Banks: www.sydneybanks.org.
Three Principles Foundation: www.threeprinciplesfoundation.org.

MGI in Context of Education Theory and Related Research

The *MGI* comprehensive Pre-K-12 curriculum was developed to complement evidence based approaches to effective education and fostering student resilience. *MGI* theory stands on the shoulders of significant educational and other relevant researchers such as, but not limited to: Bonnie Benard, Faye Brownlie, Robert Coles, Richard Davidson, Cheryl Dweck, Jenni Donohoo, Michael Fullan, John Hattie, Ann Masten, Parker Palmer, Michael Rutter, Leyton Schnellert, George Villiant, Roger Weissberg, Emmy Werner, Steven and Sybil Wolin.

In every country there are experts dedicated to bringing out the best in students. For example, with leadership of Kathy Marshall Emerson, the National Resilience Resource Center sees every youth as at promise rather than as at risk.

MGI focuses on simple principles operating in all students. Its objectives point to the promise inside every student to: **(1)** enhance Personal Well-being, and **(2)** develop Communication, Thinking, Social Emotional Learning, and Personal and Social Responsibility competencies. These general objectives may be customized to fit specific countries, systems, schools or classrooms.

Authors Barbara Aust and Kathy Marshall Emerson, education and resilience veterans, guided *MGI* conceptual development to clarify the "fit" between *MGI* and established cutting edge global educational efforts and research. These sample resources laying out the "Big Picture" in *MGI* may be especially helpful in discovering this alignment:

- "Personal Awareness and Responsibility Competency Profiles" from British Columbia's Ministry of Education provides the basis for *MGI* learning objectives at https://curriculum.gov.bc.ca/sites/curriculum.gov.bc.ca/files/pdf/PersonalAwarenessResponsibilityCompetencyProfiles.pdf
- "Fitting in with Other Programs" at http://www.nationalresilienceresource.com/Fitting-In.html suggests how principles curriculum like *MGI* complements existing school initiatives and programs.
- "Educators Living in the Joy of Gratitude," facilitated by Kathy Marshall Emerson, includes 12 presentations by veteran educators describing learning, living and sharing the principles in schools globally for the last 40 years. Available from: www.threeprinciplessupermind.com/products/educators-living-the-joy-of-gratitude.254
- *MGI* rests on an essential research base such as "References Relevant to BC's Curriculum Assessment and Transformation" at https://curriculum.gov.bc.ca/sites/curriculum.gov.bc.ca/files/pdf/references.pdf

For a deeper examination of relevant research see selections below.

ADDITIONAL SCHOLARLY PUBLICATIONS

Education Research and Theory

Berk, L. (2007). *Development through the lifespan*. Boston: Allyn and Bacon.

Brownlie, F., & Schnellert, L. (2009). *It's all about thinking: Collaborating to support all learners*. Winnipeg, MB: Portage & Main Press.

Reclaiming Youth International. (1990). *Circle of courage*. Retrieved from https://www.starr.org/training/youth/aboutcircleofcourage

Cicchetti, D., Rappaport, I., Weissberg, R. (Eds.). (2006). *The promotion of wellness in children and adolescents*. Child Welfare League of America. Washington, D.C.: CWLA Press.

Coles, R. (1990). *The spiritual life of children*. Boston: Houghton Mifflin Company.

Donohoo, J. (2016). *Collective efficacy: How educators' beliefs impact student learning*. Thousand Oaks: Corwin Press.

Dweck, C. (2006). *Mindset: The new psychology of success*. New York, NY: Random House.

Fullan, M. (2016). *Indelible leadership: Always leave them learning*. Thousand Oaks, CA: Corwin Press.

Fullan, M. (2001). *Leading in a culture of change*. San Francisco, Jossey-Bass.

Hattie, J. (2015). The applicability of visible learning to higher education. *Scholarship of teaching and learning in psychology*, 1(1), 79-91.

Hattie, J. (2011). *Visible learning for teachers: Maximizing impact on learning*. New York, NY: Routledge.

Hattie, J. (2009). *Visible learning: A synthesis of over 800 meta-analyses relating to achievement*. New York, NY: Routledge.

Palmer, P. (1998). *The courage to teach: Exploring the inner landscape of a teacher's life*. San Francisco: Jossey-Bass Publishing.

Roehlkepartain, E., King, P., Wagener, L., & Benson, P. (Eds.). (2006). *The handbook of spiritual development in childhood and adolescence*. Thousand Oaks, CA: Sage Publications.

Schnellert, L., Widdess, N., & Watson, L. (2015). I*t's all about thinking: Creating pathways for all learners in middle years*. Winnipeg, MB: Portage & Main Press.

Resilience Research and Theory

Benard, B. (2004). *Resiliency: What we have learned*. Oakland, CA: West Ed.

Benard, B. (1991). *Fostering resiliency in kids: Protective factors in the family, school, and community*. Portland, OR: Northwest Regional Educational Laboratory.

Benard, B. & Marshall, K. (1997). A framework for practice: Tapping innate resilience. *Research/Practice*, Minneapolis: University of Minnesota, Center for Applied Research and Educational Improvement, Spring, pp. 9-15.

Davidson, R. J., & Begley, S. (2012). *The emotional life of your brain: How its unique patterns affect the way you think, feel and live – How you can change them.* New York: Hudson Street Press.

Marshall, K. (2004). Resilience research and practice: National Resilience Resource Center bridging the gap. In H. C. Waxman, Y. N. Padron and J. Gray (Eds.). *Educational resiliency: student, teacher, and school perspectives.* Pp. 63-84. Greenwich, CT: Information Age Publishing.

Marshall, K. (November, 1998). Reculturing systems with resilience/health realization. *Promoting positive and healthy behaviors in children: Fourteenth annual Rosalynn Carter symposium on mental health policy.* Atlanta, GA: The Carter Center, pp. 48-58.

Masten, A. (2014). *Ordinary magic: Resilience processes in development.* New York, NY: Guilford Press.

Rutter, M. (1990). Psychosocial resilience and protective mechanisms. In D. Ciccetti, A. Masten, K. Neuchterlein, J. Rolf, & S. Weintraub (Eds.), *Risk and protective factors in the development of psychopathology* (pp.181-214). New York: Cambridge University Press.

Shapiro, S. & Carlson, L. (2009). *The art and science of mindfulness: Integrating mindfulness into psychology and the helping professions.* Washington, DC: American Psychological Association.

Sternberg, E., (2001). *The balance within: The science connecting health and emotions.* New York, NY: W.H. Freeman & Co.

Vaillant, G. (2012). *Triumphs of experience: The men of the Harvard grant study.* Cambridge: The Belknap Press of Harvard University Press.

Werner, E. & Smith, R., (2001). *Journeys from childhood to midlife: Overcoming the odds.* Ithaca, NY: Cornell University Press.

Werner, E. (2005). What can we learn about resilience from large-scale longitudinal studies? In S. Goldstein & R. Brooks (Eds.), *Handbook of resilience in children* (91-106). New York, NY: Kluwer Academic/Plenum.

Wolin, S.J. & Wolin, S. (1993). *The resilient self: How survivors of troubled families rise above adversity.* New York, NY: Villard Books

Three Principles in Education

Aust, B. (2016). Field notes: Capturing the moment with a story. *ASCD Express.* from www.ascd.org/ascd-express/vol12/1207-aust.aspx

Aust, B. (2013). *The essential curriculum: 21 ideas for developing a positive and optimistic culture.* Author.

Aust, B., & Vine, W. (2003, October). The power of voice in schools. *ASCD Classroom Leadership,* 7, 5, 8.

Campsall, C. (2005). Increasing student sense of feeling safe: The role of thought and common sense in developing social responsibility. Unpublished master's thesis. Royal Roads University, Victoria, British Columbia, Canada.

Marshall Emerson, K. (2015). "Resilience research and community practice: A view from the bridge." Paper presented to the Pathways to Resilience III, 6/19/2015, Halifax, Nova Scotia.

Marshall, K. (2005, September). Resilience in our schools: Discovering mental health and hope from the inside-out. In D. L. White, M. K. Faber, & B. C. Glenn (Eds.). *Proceedings of Persistently Safe Schools 2005*. 128-140. Washington, DC: Hamilton Fish Institute, The George Washington University for U. S. Department of Justice, Office of Juvenile Justice and Delinquency Prevention.

Roots of *MGI*

MGI is the first principles-based comprehensive school curriculum. The earliest educators to quietly carry the principles into their schools—Barbara Aust and Christa Campsall—began learning from Sydney Banks in 1975 in British Columbia. Jane Tucker, Bob Campsall and Marika Mayer also began to learn from Sydney Banks in the mid-1970's and all have worked in schools directly with students for many years. By 1993 Kathy Marshall Emerson of the National Resilience Resource Center was integrating the principles in two 20-year school community projects in America. By 2016 the *Educators Living in the Joy of Gratitude* global webinar series documented the experiences of veteran Pre-K- 12 educators sharing the principles "inside the schoolhouse."

The outcomes of learning, living and then sharing the principles in education complement many efforts to effectively transform education at all levels. There is growing interest in integrating the principles in education globally. To be successful these efforts must be in alignment with applicable, current curriculum standards in any location; in some cases widely accepted research-based papers provide the bests guidance. Most countries have easily accessible guidelines. These are samples:

American Common Core State Standards Initiative. (2017). *About the Standards*. Retrieved from www.corestandards.org.

BC Ministry of Education. (2016). Curriculum. *BC's New Curriculum*. Retrieved from www.curriculum.gov.bc.ca/curriculum-updates.

BC Ministry of Education. (2016). *Personal Awareness and Responsibility Competency Profiles*. Retrieved from https://curriculum.gov.bc.ca/sites/curriculum.gov.bc.ca/files/pdf/PersonalAwarenessResponsibilityCompetencyProfiles.pdf

"Collaborative for Academic, Social, and Emotional Learning (CASEL). (2017)." *Core SEL Competencies*. Retrieved from http://www.casel.org/core-competencies/

"Personal, Social, Health and Economic (PSHE) Education." *Gov.UK*. Retrieved from http://www.gov.uk

"Promoting Fundamental British Values as part of SMSC in Schools" (2014). *Gov.UK*. Retrieved from http://www.gov.uk

"Secondary National Curriculum." 02 Dec. (2014). *Gov.UK*. Retrieved from http://www.gov.uk

United Kingdom, HM Government. (January, 2017). The Government's Response to the Five Year Forward View for Mental Health. Retrieved from https://www.gov.uk/government/uploads/system/uploads/attachment_data/file/582120/FYFV_mental_health_government_response.pdf

United Kingdom, HM Government. (December 2017). Transforming Children and Young People's Mental Health Provision: Provision of a Green Paper. Presented to Parliament by Secretaries of Departments of Health and for Education from https://www.gov.uk/government/uploads/system/uploads/attachment_data/file/664855/Transforming_children_and_young_people_s_mental_health_provision.pdf

Instructional Materials for Pre K – 12 Learners
ed-talks.com

My Guide Inside® Pre-K -12 Comprehensive Curriculum

Campsall, C. with Marshall Emerson, K. (2018). *My Guide Inside, Learner Book I*, Charleston, SC: Create Space Independent Publishing Platform.

Campsall, C. with Marshall Emerson, K. (2018). *My Guide Inside, Teacher Manual, Book I*, Charleston, SC: Create Space Independent Publishing Platform.

Campsall, C., Tucker, J. (2017). *My Guide Inside, Learner Book II*, Charleston, SC: Create Space Independent Publishing Platform.

Campsall, C. with Marshall Emerson, K. (2017). *My Guide Inside, Teacher Manual, Book II*, Charleston, SC: Create Space Independent Publishing Platform.

Campsall, C. with Marshall Emerson, K. (2017). *My Guide Inside, Learner Book III*, Charleston, SC: Create Space Independent Publishing Platform.

Campsall, C., with Marshall Emerson, K. (2017). *My Guide Inside, Teacher Manual Book III*, San Charleston, SC: Create Space Independent Publishing Platform.

EPUB
Please Note: For school administrators who purchase classroom packages (*MGI I, II or III*), a free EPUB file will be provided with license agreements. Contact ed-talks.com

Supplemental Children's Picture Book
Campsall, C., Tucker, J. (2017). *Whooo ... has a Guide Inside?* Charleston, SC: Create Space Independent Publishing Platform.

Acknowledgments

Sydney Banks deeply cared about young people. He knew that if we could help our youth, the world would be "a far, far better place." He was an ordinary man who had an experience that profoundly changed him from the inside-out. For the rest of his life, as a speaker and author, he was dedicated to sharing the universal Three Principles he uncovered: Mind, Consciousness and Thought.

As teachers, school administrators and other helping professionals learned these principles, they consistently reported unusually positive results with youth and adults in schools, mental health clinics, businesses, jails and community agencies. The principles *MGI* shares focus on individuals discovering their natural inner wisdom and innate mental health. This understanding is now gaining international recognition and respect. We can all be so grateful for the opportunity to explore the principles' profound life-changing message of hope.

Heartfelt thanks go to the team of volunteer dedicated professionals who assisted me in creating *MGI*. Jane Tucker, who co-authored the intermediate edition of *My Guide Inside*, assisted in major ways with this teen edition by contributing Lenny's and Lilianna's stories, as well as influencing the text and stories with her insightful suggestions. Her boundless goodwill for sharing her understanding has enriched this curriculum immensely.

Tom Tucker artfully produced the cover and this format and Jo Aucoin created our special owl graphic. Psychiatrist Bill Pettit created his personal letter because he firmly believes pointing young people to their *Guide Inside* restores mental health. Elsie Spittle and Dr. George Pransky, in collaboration with practitioners, created *Sharing the Principles of Mind, Consciousness, and Thought*, included here as a valuable resource.

As author, school teacher and principal, Barb Aust, over forty years, saw the principles bring out the best in students and teachers. She and Kathy Marshall Emerson of the National Resilience Resource Center reviewed extensively and provided important links between the principles, curriculum guidelines, and sound research regarding education, resilience, and related fields. Kathy initially strongly encouraged me to undertake this curriculum and, behind the scenes assisted me extensively in co-creating this *MGI* Teacher Manual and the Learner Book.

Braden Hughs, a school social worker, shared his candle metaphor with us, social worker Mavis Karn contributed her "secret" letter and Paul Lock, trainer and coach, offered his poem and artwork. My husband Bob Campsall contributed insights, school stories, and encouraged me every step of the way. Our son, Michael, created the accompanying website for *MGI*. For all teens and adult reviewers who offered their suggestions and moved *MGI* along, many, many thanks!

–The Author

Overview of My Guide Inside Comprehensive Curriculum

About the Authors

Christa Campsall (right) is a pioneer in bringing the Three Principles to Pre-K-12 education. Since 1975, this has been the foundation of her work as a classroom teacher, special education teacher and School-Based Team Chair. Christa was mentored by Sydney Banks and received certification from him to teach Three Principles. She has a BEd and DiplSpEd from University of British Columbia, and a MA from Royal Roads University. She and her husband live on Salt Spring Island, British Columbia.

Kathy Marshall Emerson (left), National Resilience Resource Center founding director, facilitates long-term school community principle–based training and systems change. Her free and globally available recorded webinar series, Educators Living in the Joy of Gratitude, features international veteran educators' outcomes of sharing the principles for as much as forty years in classrooms, school systems, and student services. She has a MA from the University of Southern California and is adjunct faculty at the University of Minnesota.

My Guide Inside is a three-part comprehensive Pre-K-12 story-based curriculum covering developmentally appropriate topics in an ongoing process of learning throughout the entire school career. As a teacher, you choose the level of *My Guide Inside* that is just right for your students in your particular school system: **Book I** (introduction, primary), **Book II** (continuation, intermediate) and **Book III** (advanced, secondary). With this comprehensive curriculum, school leaders will be able to chart a continuous instructional plan to share the Three Principles with students as they move through the grades.

Objectives of *My Guide Inside* (Book II): The principles discussed in this learner book operate in all people, including every student. This *MGI* curriculum points the way to wholeness, happiness, creativity and well-being in all parts of life. Therefore, *MGI* has these two globally appropriate academic goals to: **(1)** Enhance Personal Well-being with an understanding of these principles, and **(2)** Develop competencies in Communication, Thinking, and Personal and Social Responsibility. *MGI* accomplishes both goals by using stories, discussion and various written and creative activities, as the learning increases your students' competency in English Language Arts and several other areas.

Discovering their *Guide Inside* is key to learning and enhances students' ability to make decisions, navigate life and build healthy relationships. Accessing that natural wisdom will affect well-being, spiritual wellness, personal and social responsibility, and positive personal and cultural identity. Social emotional learning, including self-determination, self-regulation and self-efficacy, are also natural outcomes of greater awareness.

This *MGI Teacher's Manual* accompanies *My Guide Inside Learner Book II*. The student book, under separate title, offers a hopeful, simple way for learners to become aware of how they operate mentally from the inside-out. This understanding maximizes personal well-being and improves school climate, learner behavior and academic performance.

The *MGI Teacher's Manual* contains lesson plans, pre- and post-assessments, activities, evaluation scales and resources. We introduce universal principles making this curriculum for global use with all learners. In addition, we reference curriculum guidelines from Canada, the United Kingdom, and the United States.

> • *MGI* meets selected requirements for *English Language Arts, Health Education, Career Education and Personal, Social, Health and Economic Education.*
> • *MGI* supports inclusion and develops *Communication, Social Emotional Learning, Personal Well-being Awareness, Social Responsibility and Thinking* competencies.

MGI Book II is appropriate for all learners in any intermediate classroom, older learners on a modified program, home learners, self-directed learners working independently, individual learners in counseling or personal coaching and in discussions with parents. Reading Level is "Easy to Read." Ideal age is 9-12, usually intermediate level. Most importantly this comprehensive curriculum offers a flexible framework to customize, adapt or modify to fit each teacher's understanding of the principles and the needs of students.

My Guide Inside® is available through ed-talks.com
For additional information, contact Christa Campsall: christa@ed-talks.com

What Professionals Say About My Guide Inside

"This beautifully composed curriculum is a must for school principals, teachers, and teacher assistants. It points educators and their students towards a natural and inner state of well-being. All participants are given multiple opportunities to become learners in a state of joy and to access their common sense and innate wisdom in all areas of life. *My Guide Inside* is a holistic approach with the essence of our humanity at its core."

Dean Rees-Evans, MSc
Teacher, Researcher, Well-being Mentor, Macksville, New South Wales, AU

"Parents and teachers alike will find this a helpful resource as they work with children and youth to find the wisdom that lies inside each one of them, and to develop strategies for solving problems with the help of their own special guide."

Kelda Logan, MA
Principal, Salt Spring Island, BC, CA

"These authentic stories are simple, yet profound, and have the capacity to lead students to their *Guide Inside*."

Barb Aust, BEd, MEd
Principal, Education Consultant and Author, Salt Spring Island, BC, CA

"I have been incredibly lucky to have personally known Sydney Banks and to have been raised surrounded by the Three Principles, which have remained at the heart of my approach as an educator. I have been a teacher in inner city schools in Baltimore, Miami and the Bronx for over 12 years. By sharing the simple understanding that students are able to decide how they wish to experience life through their choices about thought, I have seen aggressive students become peacemakers, shy, self-conscious children become confident leaders, and the level of consciousness and empathy raised in an entire school. I am thrilled that this curriculum will be seen and experienced by so many! This understanding has the power to change education and the school experience on a global scale!"

Christina G. Puccio, Mentor Teacher/Coach
PS 536, Bronx, N.Y.

"*My Guide Inside* brings children and youth into contact with their own wisdom. Christa and Jane remind readers about the power of our thinking and support us to practice 'knowing' through listening. The beautiful tapestry of stories helps readers to 'think and see clearly.' This book is an extraordinary resource…a gift for us all."

Nia Williams, MA
Guidance Counselor, Gulf Islands, BC, CA

"As a teacher with many years' experience working with children and teens, including high risk who, for many reasons, did not fare well in the education system, I welcome this inspiring curriculum with great appreciation and respect. At last, here is a different conversation available for schools, one that teaches a simple and straightforward path to securing emotional stability and healthy states of mind. This is the missing piece education so dearly needs."

Sue Pankiewicz, BA, PGCE
Former Senior Teacher for Special Education Unit,
Education Consultant, Colchester, UK

"As a headteacher (principal) for over thirty years, I have often witnessed first-hand the restless struggles many children and youth experience as they begin to feel comfortable in their own skin. Christa and Jane's straightforward, simple but profound curriculum helps teachers to point youth in a different direction, to our *Guide Inside*, our essence, our wisdom. I would recommend this guide to teachers as a powerful source of support. It helps us all remember who we really are … pure love."

Peter Anderson, Cert. Edn. Adv. Diploma (Cambridge)
Three Principles Facilitator, Headteacher Advisor, Essex, UK

Made in the USA
Monee, IL
06 March 2020